Animals of the World

Tarantula

By Edana Eckart

A Division of Scholastic Inc.
New York / Toronto / London / Auckland / Sydney
Mexico City / New Delhi / Hong Kong
Danbury, Connecticut

Photo Credits: Cover © Royalty Free/Corbis; p. 5 © Robert Holmes/Corbis; p. 7 © Mary Clay/Getty Images; p. 9 © Eric and David Hosking/Corbis; p. 11 © Galen Rowell/Corbis; p. 13 © Planet Earth/Care Farneti/Getty Images; p. 15 © ABPL Image Library/Animals Animals; pp.17, 19 © Michael & Patricia Fogden/Corbis; p. 21 © Ronnie Kaufman/Corbis
Contributing Editor: Shira Laskin
Book Design: Christopher Logan

Library of Congress Cataloging-in-Publication Data

Eckart, Edana.
    Tarantula / by Edana Eckart.
    p. cm. — (Animals of the world)
    Includes index
    ISBN 0-516-25051-5 (lib. bdg.) — ISBN 0-516-25167-8 (pbk.)
    1. Tarantulas — Juvenile literature. I. Title.

    QL458.42.T5E34 2005
    595.4'4—dc22

                                        2004002337

Contents

A **tarantula** is a **spider**.

There are more than eight hundred kinds of tarantulas.

Most tarantulas are brown or black.

Some of them are very colorful.

Tarantulas have eight legs.

Their bodies are covered in hair.

Tarantulas live all over
the world.

Most tarantulas live
in **rain forests**.

11

Some tarantulas make their homes in the **soil**.

Other tarantulas live in trees or under rocks.

Tarantulas eat **insects** such as **crickets**.

15

Tarantulas bite insects to **poison** them.

This makes the insects easier to eat.

Baby tarantulas come from eggs.

A mother tarantula lays her eggs in a **cocoon**.

eggs inside cocoon

19

Some people keep tarantulas as pets.

Tarantulas are very interesting animals.

21

New Words

cocoon (kuh-**koon**) a covering made from silky
threads produced by some animals to protect
themselves or their eggs

crickets (**krik**-its) jumping insects similar
to grasshoppers

insects (**in**-sekts) very small animals that have three
pairs of legs and a pair of antennae on their
heads, which they use to feel

poison (**poi**-zuhn) a substance used by tarantulas
to kill the animals they eat

rain forests (**rayn for**-ists) dense, tropical forests
where a lot of rain falls

soil (**soil**) the top layer of Earth that we plant
things in

spider (**spide**-uhr) a small animal with eight legs
and no wings

tarantula (tuh-**ran**-chuh-luh) a large, hairy spider
found mainly in warm regions

To Find Out More

Books
Bug Books: Tarantula
by Monica Harris
Heinemann Library

Tarantula Spiders
by James E. Gerholdt
Checkerboard Library

Web Site
Tarantulas
http://www.enchantedlearning.com/subjects/arachnids/
    spider/Tarantulaprintout.shtml
Learn about tarantulas and paint a picture of a tarantula
on this Web site.

Index

About the Author
Edana Eckart is a freelance writer. She has written many books about animals.

Reading Consultants
Kris Flynn, Coordinator, Small School District Literacy, The San Diego County Office of Education

Shelly Forys, Certified Reading Recovery Specialist, W.J. Zahnow Elementary School, Waterloo, IL

Paulette Mansell, Certified Reading Recovery Specialist, and Early Literacy Consultant, TX